MORE THAN JUST A GAME

The Black Origins of Basketball

Madison Moore

illustrated by
Lonnie Ollivierre

Albert Whitman & Company
Chicago, Illinois

On cracked blacktops and driveways,
on laminated floors in echoing gyms,
and on NBA courts across the United States,
black and brown skin shines, sweaty
and pushing toward that next crisp *swish*!

More than 70 percent of current players in the National Basketball Association are Black, crossing and juking, laughing and panting in the country's biggest arenas.

But how did they get the chance to step onto that stage?

They earned it.

Played for it.

Made it their game.

When basketball was invented, not everyone was welcome on the court.

In 1891 in Springfield, Massachusetts, James Naismith hung a peach basket in a YMCA gym, grabbed a soccer ball, and posted thirteen rules on the wall.

The sport spread like wildfire. Basketball was fun and easy to learn. But lots of people didn't get the chance to join in. It was uncommon at this time for girls to play any sports at all.

The game moved through segregated YMCAs and privileged colleges, evolving and changing in spaces that Black Americans were not widely allowed to go.

So they made their own spaces.

In 1904, Edwin Bancroft Henderson, a Black gym teacher in Washington, DC, learned the game at an open Harvard summer course for teachers. He brought it back to his city. He taught his students to dribble and dish, float and shoot.

The students took it to their neighborhoods, crossed over cousins and brothers—feet pounding on cement.

Still, basketball couldn't catch like wildfire for Black players no matter how much they liked the sport. When winter hit or schools closed, there was no place to play. But the early 1900s were bringing on a Black cultural revolution, and it was the perfect chance for the love of basketball to take root, spread deep, and flourish.

Early vinyl records were making Black musical styles, like jazz, ragtime, and blues, popular across the country. New dance halls and ballrooms opened for Black musicians to perform, drawing swaying and swinging crowds.

Basketball supporters in cities like New York and Chicago saw an opportunity in these musical spaces. They made deals with the owners of dance halls.

A few hours before musicians arrived to take the stage, players showed up to hoop. Crowds switched from alley-oops to eight-count steps, all at the drop of a beat. Through this marriage of basketball and dance, the sport was becoming more than just a game.

Crowds socialized as they watched and cheered on each glorious game. Both old and young were on their feet and moving, uplifted and united by basketball.

In the 1910s and 1920s, Black teams started to organize. Churches, park districts, youth organizations, and community centers all across the country hosted leagues and tournaments that grew more and more competitive. Teams from historically Black colleges traveled long distances to play one another.

White colleges had been competing against one another for many years, and white professional club teams existed in most major cities.

But now, Black teams were rising to meet them on the court, ready to shake up thirty years of segregated playing.

These teams were known as the Black Fives—all-Black club teams that put five men on the court to take the ball from fingertip to net, to break ankles, to shoot, score, and win!

In Pittsburgh, the Monticello Athletic Association was home to Cumberland Posey, widely accepted as the best Black player of the Black Fives generation.

In Chicago, the Savoy Big Five drew crowds to the South Side's Savoy Ballroom, building on the history of basketball and dance to bring more people to the sport. A few years later, they split into two, forming a new team called the Harlem Globetrotters— the original namesake of the modern-day exhibition team.

In New York, the Renaissance, often called the Rens, won 2,588 of 3,117 games across twenty-five years—an unmatched winning rate of 83 percent.

These teams brought Black excellence to a new scale. Though not many people today know the names of the Black players of the 1920s and 1930s, anyone who cared about basketball in that time had to recognize the skills of these self-made Black players.

Basketball still didn't have one standard league across the country, but the Black Fives played against one another and against some all-white teams in different games and tournaments.

Still, many tournaments remained completely closed off to Black teams, and teams that had both Black and white players were extremely rare.

Then in 1939 an annual tournament called the World Championship of Professional Basketball began.

Despite the large number of successful Black Fives teams, the first selection committee only invited two Black teams to compete.

But these teams had been beating the odds for decades.

In a landmark victory, in a stadium packed with white fans, the Rens, led by tournament MVP Clarence "Puggy" Bell, defeated the all-white Oshkosh All-Stars and claimed the first-ever professional basketball world championship.

In 1940 the Harlem Globetrotters took home the title in a one-shot-lead victory.

In 1943 the Washington Bears rose to the top in a double-digit win.

Black players were proving, over and over again, that basketball was their sport.

They wouldn't be left out.

They couldn't be overlooked.

The NBA officially formed in 1949, and within one year, it transitioned into an integrated league, recognizing that the only way forward for men's basketball was to include everyone.

This was a victory, but still not for all. Players from the Black Fives era were widely left out of basketball's Hall of Fame. Black coaches and owners were excluded from managing the new NBA teams.

The Black Fives faded from the history of the sport. The name Cumberland Posey may have been forgotten, but without him, there would be no Michael Jordan. Without Puggy Bell, we'd have no LeBron James.

The Black Fives made the sport we celebrate today, and used it to change their communities.

Basketball's uniquely Black history echoes in the squeak of each sneaker and the cheers of each fan, inspiring a new wave of dreams and determination in the hands of each player that picks up a ball today.

Black Fives Player Profiles

Cumberland W. Posey Jr.

From 1920 to 1925, Cumberland W. Posey Jr. was considered the best active Black basketball player. While playing with Pittsburgh's Loendi Big Five, he won five Colored Basketball World Championships. In 2016 he was inducted into the Naismith Memorial Basketball Hall of Fame.

Zachary Clayton

Zachary Clayton won two World Championship of Professional Basketball titles, with the New York Rens and the Washington Bears, and was enshrined in the Philadelphia Basketball Hall of Fame in 1989. More than twenty years later, in 2017, he was inducted into the Naismith Memorial Basketball Hall of Fame.

Edwin B. Henderson

Edwin B. Henderson, also called the "Grandfather of Black Basketball," introduced basketball to Black communities on a widespread scale. He also created sustainable infrastructure for the game, including the first black athletic conference. In 2013 he was inducted into the Naismith Memorial Basketball Hall of Fame.

Clarence "Puggy" Bell

Clarence "Puggy" Bell was the MVP of the New York Rens for nine straight seasons, including during their victory at the inaugural World Championship of Professional Basketball Tournament in 1939. He was also named MVP of the championship that year. In 2005 he was enshrined in the New York Basketball Hall of Fame, but he is still awaiting induction into the Naismith Memorial Basketball Hall of Fame.

Basketball Greats Player Profiles

Michael Jordan

Michael Jordan won six NBA titles in six attempts with the Chicago Bulls, from 1991–1998. He holds five league MVP awards and six Finals MVP awards, and is widely considered the greatest basketball player of all time.

Bill Russell

With the Boston Celtics, Bill Russell won eleven NBA titles, more than any other player in NBA history. He is considered the greatest defensive player of all-time.

Wilt Chamberlain

Wilt Chamberlain holds two NBA titles, four league MVP awards, and one Finals MVP award. In his 1961–62 NBA season with the Lakers, he averaged 50.4 points and 25.7 rebounds. In 1962 he scored 100 points in one game.

Magic Johnson

Magic Johnson holds five NBA titles, three league MVP awards, and three Finals MVP awards. In his fourteen-year career with the Lakers, from 1979–1993, he made nine trips to the NBA Finals.

Black Fives Foundation

Though the stories of the Black Fives players and teams may not be widely known, there are many people working to honor and preserve the legacies of these basketball greats.

One of these organizations is the Black Fives Foundation, started by Claude Johnson in 2013. The foundation works to maintain an archive of memorabilia, historical accounts,

and photos from the Black Fives era. It also advocates for recognition of pioneering Black Fives players by researching their careers and bringing attention to their successes. Since its start, the foundation has succeeded in helping nine players, including one woman, get enshrined in the Naismith Memorial Basketball Hall of Fame, which has enshrined more than four hundred players globally. The Black Fives Foundation continues to work to get more players honored.

The history is much larger than the story told here; female players have their own history and achievements, and Black players continue to make basketball history every day.

To learn more about the Black Fives era or to support the Black Fives Foundation, visit www.blackfives.org.

Selected Sources

Adler, Margot. "Before the NBA Was Integrated, We Had the Black Fives." NPR, March 15, 2014. https://www.npr.org/sections/codeswitch/2014/03/15/290117181/before-the-nba-was-integrated-we-had-the-black-fives.

Black Fives Foundation. "Black Fives Foundation Home." Last modified January 4, 2015, https://www.blackfives.org/.

Sandomir, Richard. "Remembering the 'Black Fives' of Pro Basketball." *New York Times*, March 19, 2014. https://www.nytimes.com/2014/03/20/arts/artsspecial/remembering-the-black-fives-of-pro-basketball.html.

For my dad; I hope this makes up for my (lack of) basketball skills.
—MM

To my mom, Victoria Griffith—
without you nothing I do will be possible. Thank you!
—LO

Library of Congress Cataloging-in-Publication data
is on file with the publisher.

Text copyright © 2021 by Madison Moore
Illustrations copyright © 2021 by Albert Whitman & Company
Illustrations by Lonnie Ollivierre
First published in the United States of America
in 2021 by Albert Whitman & Company

ISBN 978-0-8075-5271-1 (hardcover)
ISBN 978-0-8075-5272-8 (ebook)

Printed in China
10 9 8 7 6 5 4 3 2 WKT 26 25 24 23 22

Design by Rick DeMonico

For more information about Albert Whitman & Company,
visit our website at www.albertwhitman.com.